GUIDANCE NOTE ON STATE-OWNED ENTERPRISE REFORM FOR NONSOVEREIGN AND ONE ADB PROJECTS

NOVEMBER 2022

ADB

ASIAN DEVELOPMENT BANK

Contents

Tables and Boxes

Acknowledgments

This guidance note was prepared by David Robinett, senior public management specialist (State-Owned Enterprise Reforms), and Richard Frederick (consultant) under the auspices of the Asian Development Bank's State-Owned Enterprise Working Group, chaired by Hiranya Mukhopadhyay, chief of Governance Thematic Group, Sustainable Development and Climate Change Department.

Special thanks to the following staff for their advice and comments: Craig Roberts, Catherine Marsh, Donald Lambert, Levan Mtchedlishvili, Mayank Choudhary, Peter Ho, Andrew McCartney, Shinya Kondo, Fiona Alpe, and Yurendra Basnett. We would also like to thank the following for their support: Toni Figurasin and Aly Escandor.

Abbreviations

ADB	Asian Development Bank
CEO	chief executive officer
DMC	developing member country
ESG	environmental, social, and governance
KPI	key performance indicator
IFRS	International Financial Reporting Standards
NSO	nonsovereign operation
OECD	Organisation for Economic Co-operation and Development
OP6	Operational Priority 6
PSOD	Private Sector Operations Department
PSO	public sector obligation
RPT	related party transaction
SOE	state-owned enterprise
TA	technical assistance

About This Guidance Note

Strategy 2030 and Operational Priority 6 commits the Asian Development Bank (ADB) to support state-owned enterprise (SOE) reform in its developing member countries (DMCs). This guidance note is designed to guide ADB staff in their work with SOEs, including in nonsovereign and One ADB projects and through related technical assistance (TA). It covers potential risks for such projects, and mitigating reforms that may be initiated during the lead up to or during processing, including as part of earlier sovereign projects, programs, or TA.

The guidance note reviews the significance of SOEs in Asia and the Pacific and for the work of ADB, the definition of SOEs, and the role of SOE reform and nonsovereign lending to SOEs in ADB's strategy and relevant requirements. It reviews the challenges that SOEs face and how these impact their access to commercial finance without a sovereign guarantee. The longest part of the guidance note discusses how to mitigate these challenges in the context of ADB nonsovereign projects. It identifies broader reforms that can make SOE borrowers more creditworthy and capable of accessing funds without a sovereign guarantee, or accessing those funds on better terms. The guidance note also addresses One ADB projects that combine staff with private and public sector expertise and concludes with additional guidance for ADB staff on how to incorporate SOE reform into their projects and programs. In addition, it provides further resources for staff working on SOE reform.

Although intended for ADB staff, this guidance note may also be of use to DMC officials and SOE boards and management interested in SOE reform and helping SOEs access commercial finance, in which case its most effective use would be in conjunction with other materials cited here.

Introduction

State-owned enterprises (SOEs) have long played an important role in the developing economies of Asia and the Pacific. They remain dominant in areas with some of the highest development impact: energy, water, and transport, including passenger rail, ports, and airports. In many Asia and Pacific economies, SOEs are either the primary or sole provider of these vital goods and services, or the key counterparts of service delivery through contracting with the private sector or public–private partnerships. Globally, SOEs account for 55% of infrastructure investment in middle- and lower-income economies.[1] State-owned banks and financial institutions also make up a large part of the financial systems in Asia and the Pacific, holding 40% or more of banking system assets in a number of countries.[2]

In Asia and the Pacific, governments traditionally financed most SOEs directly or through sovereign guarantees that made SOE borrowing the equivalent of government debt. However, in recent decades, a growing number of SOEs have turned to capital markets and private lenders to finance their investment on commercial terms. Hundreds of SOEs are now listed on the world's stock exchanges and include many of the largest publicly listed companies in Asia and the Pacific. Commercial debt issued by SOEs approaches $1.5 trillion, and this does not include bank lending made on commercial terms.[3]

SOEs hold significant public assets, and SOE dividends can be a key source of public revenue. At the same time, SOEs may have substantial liabilities that require government guarantees or on-lending through the government, adding to the national debt. If poorly managed, they can also impose a serious fiscal drain if governments are required to provide financial support through ongoing equity injections, loans, or subsidies. Overall, SOE debt can be as high as 50% of overall public sector debt, and as much as 20% of gross domestic product in some countries.[4]

These large liabilities are one reason that governments are increasingly pushing SOEs to borrow on commercial terms. Borrowing without a sovereign guarantee helps create fiscal space for the government and leaves their liabilities lower than they otherwise would be, while giving the SOE a new way to finance needed investments. Accessing capital markets and other private sector finance also subject SOEs to greater oversight. Crucially, accessing commercial finance typically requires substantial SOE reform that may bring other benefits to SOE governance and performance. For these reasons, a growing number of Organisation for Economic Co-operation and Development (OECD) countries limit or prohibit SOEs borrowing with sovereign guarantees. Multilateral development banks, including the Asian Development Bank (ADB), have also put greater emphasis on lending to SOEs through nonsovereign modalities that preclude sovereign guarantees (footnote 4).

[1]   World Bank. 2017. *Who Sponsors Infrastructure Projects? Disentangling Public and Private Contributions.* Washington, DC.
[2]   International Monetary Fund. 2020. *Fiscal Monitor.* Washington, DC.
[3]   ADB. 2021. *The Bankable SOE: Commercial Financing for State-Owned Enterprises.* Manila.
[4]   ADB. 2021. *Guidance Note on State-Owned Enterprise Reform in Sovereign Projects and Programs.* Manila.

ADB has always worked with SOEs in its developing member countries (DMCs), and SOE reform remains an important part of ADB's strategy. This includes substantial operational work in energy, water, and transport as well as finance, and sometimes other sectors like agriculture or communications. ADB also supports broader SOE reform and related sector reform through its policy-based lending (PBL) and technical assistance (TA). Much of this lending is provided as a sovereign guarantee through DMC governments—which is the focus of a previous guidance note (footnote 4). ADB also makes loans directly to more commercial SOEs without a guarantee, primarily through its Private Sector Operations Department (PSOD). Between a fifth and a quarter of PSOD's lending is to SOEs on a commercial basis. This guidance note focuses on this nonsovereign lending, reform to facilitate this lending, and cases in which PSOD works jointly with ADB's regional departments to transition SOEs to nonsovereign borrowing.

ADB's Strategy for Commercial Lending to State-Owned Enterprises

Strategy 2030 commits ADB to supporting SOE reform in its DMCs. Strategy 2030 confirms the importance of this reform in lower, lower-middle, and upper middle-income economies and in small island developing states, as well as the importance of SOEs in providing many essential services in DMCs.[5] Under Strategy 2030, ADB will work to improve SOE financial management capacity and internal governance. A primary goal of these reforms is to allow SOEs to access finance on commercial terms. In other words, the SOE has to be as attractive an investment as a creditworthy private sector company. Hence it should be comparable in terms of financial viability and corporate governance, which impacts the ability of the SOE to credibly repay creditors and is essential for the SOE to attract equity investment.

Strategy 2030 Operational Plan for Priority 6: Strengthening Governance and Institutional Capacity (OP6) provides greater detail on the importance of SOEs in DMCs and the SOE reform that ADB will support. It confirms the importance of SOEs for service delivery and the goal of attracting commercial finance. Under OP6, ADB will support improvements to corporate governance and other steps to improve commercial orientation for SOEs. These include corporatization; that is, converting the SOE to a company with a legal form similar to a private company, encouraging capital market access and equity investment into SOEs, and shedding noncore assets.

OP6 calls for ADB to support the prudent disinvestment of state assets, when appropriate, and improving the governance and regulation of sectors where SOEs are predominant. In some cases, this can include exposing SOEs to greater competition. Critically, OP6 highlights the importance of the state measuring SOE performance, holding SOEs accountable for that performance, and improving how the state makes other major decisions in SOEs. To be successful, this reform should be underpinned by strong government ownership and support for relevant reforms.

ADB's Operational Plan for Private Sector Operations also specifically calls for PSOD to engage with SOEs and support SOE reform. "ADB will focus on targeting SOEs where there is clear government support for relevant reforms, good corporate governance, a move toward commercialization, and private participation where appropriate." The operational plan also anticipates a transition from sovereign to nonsovereign borrowing for SOEs: "A willingness to engage in markets on a commercial basis and phased graduation away from sovereign borrowing should guide ADB engagement with any SOE." This phasedown will be facilitated by ADB staff from PSOD working together with their colleagues from regional departments in One ADB teams.

Strategy 2030 also anticipates a One ADB approach. "ADB's private sector operations will draw on public sector operations to provide integrated solutions. Public sector operations (both project lending and PBL) can complement private sector operations by ... preparing SOEs for commercial financing."

---

[5] ADB. 2018. *Strategy 2030: Achieving a Prosperous, Resilient, Inclusive, and Sustainable Asia and the Pacific.* Manila.

ADB's work on SOEs is coordinated by the bank's SOE Working Group. Established in 2016, the working group focused on knowledge sharing, data collection, and supporting the now mandatory identification of all projects and programs with SOEs. It also oversaw the development of a database on 10 years of SOE engagement that has now been integrated into ADB's operations platform. The working group has now entered a new phase, focusing on direct support to ADB's operational work with SOEs.

What Are State-Owned Enterprises?

ADB defines SOEs as legal entities established to undertake commercial activities and owned fully or largely by the sovereign.[6] The OECD uses a similar definition: a "corporate entity recognized by national law as an enterprise, and in which the state exercises ownership."[7] The SOE should have a distinct legal personality from government ministries or other government bodies. These include entities with the same legal form as enterprises in the private sector, such as limited liability companies and corporations. It also includes "statutory corporations," which are SOEs founded under their own legislative act that have some revenue-earning functions.

As enterprises, SOEs are distinct from other government agencies that are either regulatory in nature or provide a public good, for example, air traffic control or funding scientific research. They are also distinct from state-owned schools and medical facilities.

SOEs can be owned solely by a national, provincial, or municipal government. They may occasionally have multiple government owners, for example, an urban transit system with national and municipal ownership, or an international pipeline owned by the governments of different nations. They may also have private investors, for example through listing on a stock exchange, or strategic investment by a private fund or company. In some cases, another SOE or a state-linked investment fund or financial institution may be an investor, either from the same or another country. This kind of cross-state ownership has become increasingly prevalent as state-linked pension funds and sovereign wealth funds have grown and large SOEs have become increasingly multinational.

"Owned largely by the sovereign" implies 50% or more direct ownership. However, indirect ownership through other SOEs and state investors should also be taken into account. As should "golden shares," special rights sometimes found in company charters and laws that give the state special veto powers over major decisions, even when they have less than 50% ownership.

This guidance note focuses on nonsovereign operations with SOEs, and SOEs capable of borrowing on commercial terms that will generally have the same legal form as private companies. SOEs capable of attracting equity investment generally must have the same form and meet the same requirements for raising outside capital. There may be exceptions—some statutory corporations with their own special legal forms do borrow without sovereign guarantees. In Asia and the Pacific, these cases are rare and should be approached carefully. On the other hand, many companies have the state or a state-linked entity, including another SOE, as a minority shareholder. This guidance note may still be relevant in those cases where the state shareholder(s) still exerts significant influence through their minority stake(s).

---

[6]   Independent Evaluation Department. 2018. *Thematic Evaluation: State-Owned Enterprise Engagement and Reform.* Manila: ADB.
[7]   OECD. 2015. *OECD Guidelines on Corporate Governance of State-Owned Enterprises.* Paris. p. 12.

Challenges and Access to Commercial Finance of State-Owned Enterprises

Any enterprise in which the managers and owners are not the same can have agency problems, particularly when the managers may have more information about the enterprise than the owners, leading to situations where conflicts of interest predominate. Modern corporate governance and the related areas of company law, corporate reporting, internal controls, and securities regulation are tools that help manage these problems in larger enterprises, especially those with many shareholders.[8]

SOEs face agency problems that are compounded by the nature of their ownership. The state acts on behalf of the people through government. In practice, for SOEs these shareholder functions may be exercised by one or more ministries and/or other government agencies. This may lead to a *complex agency chain* wherein instead of a simple conflict between management and shareholders, there are conflicts among the broader general interests, the viability of the SOE, and various political and other interests held at different points in the agency chain.

In practice, SOE challenges tend to manifest themselves in the following ways:

- **Multiple objectives and mandates.** The SOE may have a mix of formal and informal goals and targets beyond profitability and providing their primary good or service. These may not be transparent, measured effectively, or fully or even partially funded.

- **Diffuse and weak accountability.** Various parts of the government may have responsibility over the SOE or ability to influence the SOE. At the same time, there may be no clear responsibility in ensuring that the SOE stays financially viable or maintains good corporate governance. When one body is responsible for the SOE, say a ministry, this responsibility may be exercised in a way that is unclear, ad hoc, opaque, conflicted with the objectives of the SOEs, and/or lacking relevant skills. All this creates conditions for substantial political influence.

- **Unlevel playing field with the private sector.** SOEs often have both advantages in terms of subsidies and other government favors, but also the penalties noted here. They may also have special rules in terms of governance, taxation, regulation, and other areas. In many cases, these reduce accountability, competition, and performance.

- **Moral hazard.** Moral hazard, simply speaking, is a situation where a party does not fully bear the consequences of their decision making. A core problem for SOEs is that they and their management often do not face the same penalties for persistent loss-making as private sector enterprises and managers because they can anticipate financial support from the state, state-linked financial institutions, or other SOEs.

- **High levels of opacity.** SOEs often do not meet the same requirements for disclosure and transparency as that of large, privately owned companies with multiple shareholders, even though the public should be interested in their performance. Government decision-making in SOEs and the overall performance of the state-owned sector are also typically not disclosed or disclosed poorly.

---

[8] An agency problem—also known as a principal-agent problem—is one in which, in the presence of imperfect information, an agent (i.e., management) that is supposed to act in the interest of a principal (shareholders) may instead be tempted to act in their own interest.

- **Poor state-owned enterprise governance.** In addition to, and because of, the challenges noted here, other elements of SOE governance may be weak. Board members may come primarily from the government and lack relevant skills and experience. Audit and other board committees may be absent, as will performance incentives. Management and employees may be governed by civil service norms. Critically, politicians and policymakers may make decisions at various levels in the SOE in ways that tend to undermine performance. Longer-term strategy suffers, and the SOE will do a poor job in adopting to evolving challenges.

Over the last 2 decades, modern SOE reform has developed to directly address these challenges. It borrows from the corporate governance of listed companies and adds good practices specifically for SOEs. These include (i) clarifying, accounting, and paying for noncommercial mandates—typically called community service or public service obligations (PSOs); (ii) strengthening how the state acts as a shareholder, builds accountability into this function, and focuses on who carries it out; (iii) removing legal distinctions and separating policy, regulation, and ownership; (iv) encouraging a level playing field with the private sector; and (v) making SOEs comparable to leading private sector companies in terms of transparency and governance. Strong evidence is now available showing that these improvements to SOE governance increase SOE financial performance, service delivery, and fiscal impact.[9] These reforms are especially important for SOEs attempting to access commercial finance. Box 1 provides additional references on modern SOE reform.

Box 1: References and Resources for State-Owned Enterprise Reform

The Bankable SOE: Commercial Financing for State-Owned Enterprises (2021)
The definitive resource on commercial finance for state-owned enterprises (SOEs). This Asian Development Bank (ADB) study draws on a range of international good practice and provides several practical tips on how to improve SOE creditworthiness and governance to make them bankable.

Guidance Note on State-Owned Enterprise Reform in Sovereign Projects and Programs (2021)
The equivalent guidance note for projects and programs where the ADB borrower provides a sovereign guarantee. This includes more background on ADB's work with SOEs, and useful guidance for One ADB projects that include sovereign lending or require reform that goes beyond what is normally required for nonsovereign borrowers.

OECD Guidelines on Corporate Governance of State-Owned Enterprises (2015)
The international benchmark on SOE governance and reform from the Organisation for Economic Co-operation and Development (OECD). Endorsed by the members of the OECD, the guidelines were also developed and revised with substantial input from ADB's developing member countries, including through consultations at the OECD in Paris and through the Asia Network on Corporate Governance of State-Owned Enterprises.

State-Owned Enterprise Engagement and Reform: Thematic Evaluation (2018)
A review of ADB's work with SOEs by the Independent Evaluation Department.

continued on next page

---

[9]   For SOE-specific reforms: L.A. Andrés, J.L. Guasch, and S. López Azumendi. 2011. Governance in State-Owned Enterprises Revisited: The Cases of Water and Electricity in Latin America and the Caribbean. *Policy Research Working Paper*. No. 5747. Washington, DC: The World Bank; and A. Baum et al. 2019. Governance and State-Owned Enterprises: How Costly is Corruption? *IMF Working Paper*. No. 19/253. Washington, DC: International Monetary Fund. For the benefits of broader SOE reforms and fiscal impact: D. Detter. 2019. Public Commercial Assets: The Hidden Goldmine. *The Governance Brief*. Issue 40. Manila: ADB. For the benefits of corporate governance reform more generally in DMCs: S. Claessens and B. Yurtoglu. 2012. Corporate Governance and Development–An Update. *Global Corporate Governance Forum Focus 10*. Washington, DC: International Monetary Fund.

Box 1   *continued*

Corporate Governance of State-Owned Enterprises: A Toolkit (2014)
This World Bank toolkit builds on years of global engagement in DMCs. It includes in-depth guidance on both national and SOE-specific reforms.

Asia Network on Corporate Governance of State-Owned Enterprises
This network meets annually to discuss SOE reform issues and includes representatives from most ADB DMCs. Organized by the OECD with the support of the Korea Institute of Public Finance and ADB, the OECD and the network have also produced a number of publications on SOE reform.

Held by the Visible Hand: The Challenge of SOE Corporate Governance for Emerging Markets (2006)
This short paper from the World Bank gives a quick introduction to SOE challenges and reform.

Public Commercial Assets: The Hidden Goldmine (2020)
This ADB Governance Brief provides the basic steps in professionalizing the state's ownership role, setting up a specialized ownership entity, and introducing two-sided balance sheets for public commercial assets.

Labor Issues in Infrastructure Reform: A Toolkit (2004)
This toolkit by the Public–Private Infrastructure Advisory Facility Staff and World Bank gives in-depth guidance on how to manage SOE labor restructuring, including identifying surplus labor, handling severance, and helping to find new employment opportunities.

Finding Balance (2019 and earlier)
This series of reports from the ADB Private Sector Development Initiative benchmarks SOEs across Pacific economies and provides reform advice.

ADB = Asian Development Bank, DMC = developing member country, OECD = Organisation for Economic Co-operation and Development, SOE = state-owned enterprise.

Source: Authors' compilation.

ADB's Nonsovereign Operations with State-Owned Enterprises

To implement Strategy 2030 and ensure development impact, all ADB projects with SOEs have minimum requirements. The report and recommendation of the President (RRP)—the main document describing an ADB project—should describe ADB's overall engagement and reform plan, if any, for the specific entity. In addition, the RRP should note the (i) key governance and reform issues that need to be addressed for the particular SOE within the broader sector context (e.g., internal governance, financial reporting, internal audit, and disclosure) and (ii) explicit details on how the project components contribute to the overall medium to long-term SOE reform agenda.[10]

In practice, any SOE receiving finance on commercial terms, including either a nonsovereign loan or equity investment from ADB, should be very close to an investable private sector company in terms of its legal status, financial viability, corporate governance, and so forth. If there is a significant gap, then nonsovereign operations (NSO) may not be appropriate, or a One ADB approach should be taken to help transition the SOE to bankability. One ADB approaches are described below. If issues are more manageable, then focused reform may be enough to make the SOE bankable. During the ADB country programming process, PSOD and regional department staff should work together to identify potential SOEs and their governments that might be interested in moving to commercial finance and determine what sort of reforms are needed and how realistic an NSO is for the SOE.

NSO procedures are given in the *ADB Operations Manual*, section D10, and the ADB *Staff Instruction on Credit and Other Processes for Nonsovereign Operations*. In addition to confirming the "financial and economic viability" of an NSO, ADB staff must also confirm the "commitment to best practices of corporate governance" of the SOE investee. Early in the process, the ADB team must involve the Office of Risk Management "for risk relevant feedback." The subsequent due diligence process should include detailed reviews of corporate governance.

These procedures are consistent with the broader requirements for SOE reform in ADB lending. SOE-specific challenges typically manifest themselves in weak corporate governance and can undermine the broader viability of the SOE and its ability to repay creditors and ensure dividends and fair treatment of equity investors.

Risk for State-Owned Enterprises and Reform in Nonsovereign Operations

Listed here are the main areas for which SOE-related risk should be reviewed, and possible reform should be considered, for an ADB NSO, as well as upstream work to prepare for commercial borrowing. This list also does not supersede or replace required due diligence, and such due diligence is a good way to identify SOE challenges not yet addressed or recognized by the team.

---

[10]   ADB (Strategy, Policy, and Partnership Department). 2018. Alignment of Projects with Strategy 2030 – Description in the RRPs. Memorandum. 13 November (internal).

When reforms are done in parallel with processing, they can be supported with transaction TA and reinforced with appropriate financial covenants. A diverse team—including legal and financial management specialists as well as specialists and officers from the regional department and resident mission—can help in developing these reforms.

The section draws heavily on *The Bankable SOE*. This ADB publication builds on international good practice for accessing commercial finance, including the methodologies of the major credit rating agencies, and it is recommended for a more in-depth analysis of what is required for an SOE to access commercial finance. The additional references in Box 1 also give more guidance on SOE reform. This includes the *OECD Guidelines on Corporate Governance of State-Owned Enterprises*, which any SOE seeking commercial investment should largely be compliant with, and *Corporate Governance of State-Owned Enterprises: A Toolkit*, including Chapters 3–7 and Appendixes C, D, and E.

NSO transactions include both loans and equity investments from ADB. Most risks and potential reforms noted below are relevant for both commercial borrowing and equity investment. However, equity investments generally require higher standards of corporate governance, and when something is especially relevant for equity investment, this is noted. Equity can also be an especially good way to promote SOE reform. Equity investment may entitle ADB to appoint a board member and help shape the future direction of the SOE. Listing the SOE on the capital market to access equity also typically requires corporate governance and other reforms. On the other hand, for many SOEs, equity sales may not be a viable option. A more general discussion on the use of equity and commercial debt by the SOE is given under "financial structure" below.

Cash flow and financial performance

Cash flow problems at the SOE often find their root cause in mandates or regulations set by the government owner. For a regulated SOE in a sector like electricity or water, tariffs may be set too low, or some end users may pay nothing. There may be pressure to subsidize the activities of government or other SOEs through the provision of grants, loans, or guarantees or cross-subsidization of other SOEs in kind, for example provision of electricity at lower-than-normal pricing.

An SOE seeking commercial finance from an ADB NSO or another source must have sufficient cash flow. Regulated tariffs and collection must be high enough to allow payments to creditors and investors. If there is a legitimate public service obligation (PSO), this should be transparent and fully funded (as described below). Transactions with SOEs and other state bodies should be on market terms.

Financial targets for SOEs set and enforced by the SOE board, management, and or the state owner can help promote financial performance. These include measures of return on capital, such as a return on equity.[11] These ensure a positive return on invested capital, a minimum financial return to equity holders and help impose discipline and encourage efficiency in the management of the SOE. Similar targets include return on assets or return on capital invested. Profitability is also an essential indicator of economic sustainability. An SOE seeking to access commercial finance should earn a profit beyond their cost of capital. One useful measure of SOE financial performance is economic value added. This is described in more detail in Chapter IV. B. of *The Bankable SOE*.

---

[11]   These measures require proper accounting to measure relevant equity, assets, and so forth. Steps to ensure proper accounting are discussed in this section under "Disclosure."

Regular dividend payments can also help impose financial discipline on the SOE and confirm profitability. They are certainly useful for other equity investors, including ADB. Whether to pay dividends or not and what level of dividends depends on the SOE and the economic context. Some industrial sectors have predictable earnings that permit stable dividend payments while other sectors have more volatile earnings. Broadly, there are three types of dividend policies: stable, constant, and residual. *Stable* is a fixed quantity, *constant* represents a fixed percentage of earnings, and *residual* is disbursement of earnings after the SOE has paid all its capital expenditures and working capital needs. Permitting SOEs to retain earnings may be preferable when the SOE has immediate investment needs. The type and level of dividends should be negotiated between the state owner and the SOE board depending upon the situation of the SOE. An SOE seeking to improve its bankability should have a dividend policy and disclose it on its website.

Financial structure

High levels of SOE debt will undermine its ability to access commercial finance and should be a red flag for any NSO. SOE indebtedness may reflect longer-term cash flow and financial performance issues. It may be due to underinvestment in equity by the state shareholder—and sometimes ADB projects require the state shareholder to recapitalize the SOE.

SOEs can also raise equity through partial privatization. This can bring advantages outside of financing. Generally, mixed ownership and mixed financing lead to better governance, accountability, and performance. This is because listing requires SOEs to implement private sector governance standards and subjects them to the active monitoring of the capital markets. Mixed capital arrangements can help reduce the state's financing burdens, diversify its risks, and enhance its monitoring capacity.

Minority equity listings are generally less controversial compared to the sale of controlling stakes in SOEs. Where controlling stakes are sold, countries may seek to retain some decision-making powers over the SOE through golden shares or blocking minorities. These can be used to ensure that major decisions such as a change of the SOE's domicile to another country, or an alteration in the nature of the business, or large mergers and acquisitions, are subject to approval by the state. Such cautions may be warranted in some strategic industries. However, in general, the use of such instruments should be limited and should be used with caution when considered indispensable.

Public debt issues are a practical first step that can bring many of the benefits of an equity listing—though of course they do not solve the overall problem of overall indebtedness, if that is a problem. The effect on governance for bond and equity offerings is similar though the changes in governance required by bond offerings tend to be limited. Capital market rules for bond offerings focus principally on the form and content of disclosures (with, perhaps, some covenants regarding the maintenance of liquidity) while equity listings often require deep governance reforms that may, for example, impact board composition, minority shareholder protections, independence, and the control environment. Convertible debt that can allow the lender to convert to equity to capture the potential gains from a successful privatization is another option to consider as an SOE transitions to commercial finance.

Beyond the bankability of a particular SOE, both debt and equity listings can help in the development of local or regional capital markets. In some regions, the local capital markets may languish for lack of significant listings. To the extent that a DMC wishes to pursue the development of DMC capital markets, SOE offerings can present a unique opportunity to create market depth.

Focus and ownership structure

One advantage of dividend and financial targets is that they may discourage the SOE and its management from retaining funds to invest in noncore, lower returning activities. While diversification can, in theory, stabilize SOE cash flow, in practice poor performing SOEs often invest in a range of poorly performing areas outside their core functions. This sort of "empire building" is also known in the private sector, but can be worse, and more damaging, in SOEs. In some cases, it may reflect political pressures to provide benefits outside the services or goods normally provided by the SOE. It may also reflect the lack of financial incentives of SOE management, who can raise their status, and keep money from the state shareholder, by investing in a range of nonessential areas. When SOEs do this, it can create an additional problem, especially in smaller and more SOE-dominated economies. Excess SOE investment can often crowd out the private sector, exactly in those economies where private sector development should be encouraged. For all these reasons, SOEs should be encouraged to stick to their mandate, avoid investing outside of it, and spin off noncore activities when the opportunity arises.

While accessing outside equity and debt can improve SOE performance, more complex ownership structures may be subject to abuse. Such structures create considerable room for cross-subsidization that makes it difficult to assess the cost of PSOs, subsidies, and performance. The performance of affiliates and subsidiaries may not be transparent. Complex structures also increase the opportunities for undue related party transactions (RPTs). While RPTs can serve legitimate business purposes, the potential for abuse of RPTs is high enough that some credit ratings agencies discount for corporate complexity and the use of RPTs. (An approach to assigning risk to complex corporate structures is illustrated in *The Bankable SOE* in Table 4. RPTs are further discussed as follows.)

Board role and functions

The board of directors plays a pivotal role in the governance of the SOE. Good leadership and the "tone at the top" can be viewed as the foundation of any SOE's success. Boards can be either a single tier that combines both executives and nonexecutives or in two tiers with supervisory boards composed of nonexecutives that oversee a management team. Both are viable.

SOE boards should fulfill their roles and responsibilities in accord with international good practice. The key roles of a board include the following:

- Selecting the chief executive officer (CEO) and monitoring the selection of the management team.
- Monitoring the performance of the SOE, the CEO, and top executives.
- Acting as the communications link between the state and the SOE and shielding the SOE from undue interference.
- Setting strategic and tactical objectives and key performance indicators (KPIs) in coordination with the state and management.
- Ensuring that the control environment is effective, including internal and external audit, conflict of interest and ethics, and whistleblower programs.
- Ensuring that the SOE is transparent and accountable to the state, the public, and key stakeholders.
- Ensuring that the SOE's own governance including board composition, responsibilities, authorities, and decision-making thresholds reflect international good practice.

- Overseeing executive and staff development and employee morale, as well as remuneration and incentive compensation programs; and ensuring that the compensation of senior executives is aligned with financial and other KPIs.
- Ensuring that the impact of the SOE on stakeholders and the contributions of key stakeholders to the SOE receive due consideration at board level.

The first of these, CEO selection, may be the most challenging. SOE boards should play a leading role in the selection of the CEO, who should be chosen based solely on their professional qualifications. When the CEO is selected by the board—as opposed to a political selection process—they become accountable to the board, thus reducing the scope for undue political interference in SOE operations. CEOs, in turn, should have the right to constitute their own management team.

Overseeing corporate strategy is a key essential board responsibility. Frequently, boards find that they are overly occupied with mundane matters of business management at the expense of an adequate focus on strategy. Ratings agencies assess a borrower's strategy and strategy setting processes. Where the strategy-setting process is dominated by political figures, or nonbusiness professionals or weak boards, an additional level of risk may be ascribed to the SOE. Above all, the strategies themselves need to aim at ensuring the sustainability and financial health of the enterprise (Rating agency criteria for assessing any corporation's strategic positioning and risk management are illustrated in *The Bankable SOE* in Table 5).

The boards of SOEs that are established and operate under company law should exercise fiduciary duties of loyalty and care. The duty of loyalty requires acting in the interest of the SOE. This means putting personal interests aside but also implies acting in the interest of the SOE even if the interest of the majority owner conflicts with the interest of the SOE. Instructions issued by the state must, therefore, always be evaluated in terms of their impact on the financial health and viability of the SOE. This is particularly important when SOEs are required to fulfill PSOs that impose significant cost burdens. Boards should verify that PSOs do not endanger the financial sustainability of the SOE. The fiduciary duty of care means that boards must inform themselves fully regarding the issues on which they take decisions. There is a concomitant obligation of management to ensure that boards are fully informed.

SOE boards should have supporting structures and practices:

- Establish an audit committee composed primarily of independent members, at least one of whom should be an expert in accounting and auditing, or otherwise effectively oversee internal audit.
- Receive induction training covering good governance practices, in particular, roles and responsibilities, duties, strategy setting, and independence.
- Have written policies and procedures, articles, bylaws, codes, and policies to formalize the SOE's governance.
- Conduct regular meetings (but not an excessive number, which is a sign of a poor understanding of the board's role and micromanagement).
- Have the capacity to examine and understand the SOE's environmental, social, and governance (ESG) impact and devise ESG strategies.

Boards of SOEs that seek commercial finance, and especially equity investment, should also

- ensure equitable treatment of all shareholders;
- have other committees with independent members that call for oversight of areas with significant potential for conflict of interest, such as nominations, remuneration, and risk management; and
- conduct annual self-assessments of the board and the governance practices of the SOE and develop an annual remedial action plan.

Board composition and independence

Board composition should respond to the business needs of the SOE. The board should have a sufficiently diverse composition to promote genuine debate and avoid being an echo chamber. Board members should be selected based on merit. In practice, SOE board composition is often skewed heavily toward civil servants and political figures. Essential experience often missing are in business and financial knowledge, including accounting audit and risk management, private sector governance, and knowledge of ESG issues. Skills that are often missing are leadership, team building, communications, and innovation. Gender diversity may also be absent. Civil servants appointed for fixed terms may also show little interest in longer-term strategy and challenges that go beyond their tenure.

Boards should be of an adequate size (typically ranging from five to eight members). Boards that are too small may lack capacity and diversity and will not be able to staff key committees. Boards that are too large can be unwieldy or overly bureaucratic.

SOE boards should have the capacity for objective and independent decision making. The board should be able to exercise objective judgement in the interest of the SOE independently from both management and owners. Policies that support independence are (i) boards composed primarily of nonexecutive directors; (ii) the separation of the positions of CEO and board chair (in single-tier boards); (iii) a minimum number of independent board members; (iv) a formal definition of independence; and (v) disclosure of the identities of independent board members, including sufficient information for the public to make their own determination.

At a minimum, no less than two board members should be independent. A more appropriate objective is for SOE boards to be composed of no less than one-half independent members as soon as practical. All board members, even when not technically independent, should be trained in their duty to act in the interest of the SOE and to bring objective, apolitical judgement to business decisions.

Boards should be depoliticized and function without political interference. Politicization can undermine financial performance and increase reputational risks for the state. Depoliticizing boards is one of the best ways to insulate the SOE from undue political interference. It permits boards to act in a professional way, guided by commercial goals and the SOE's mandate. In general, ministers, members of Parliament, elected officials or representatives of political parties should not be eligible to become board members. Additionally, for SOEs seeking commercial finance, the number of civil servants on boards should be minimized. The use of substitutes or alternates for board members should not be allowed. Independent board members specifically should not be civil servants or chosen for their political connections.

Effective governance hinges upon achieving both autonomy and accountability. Boards should be able to fulfill their roles and responsibilities with autonomy. At the same time, boards need to be held accountable. With too little autonomy, the board or SOE management may be unable to respond to changing market conditions or use their business acumen to resolve business challenges. On the other hand, too little accountability raises the risk of corruption, imprudent investment and financing decisions, and financial loss for the SOE and the state. Autonomy and accountability are also necessary for SOE executives.

Disclosure

A major risk associated with SOEs in many countries is the poor quality of financial reporting and auditing. This may include (i) noncompliance with International Financial Reporting Standards (IFRS) or equivalent national standards; (ii) long delays in the preparation, audit, and publication of financial statements; (iii) failures to address problems identified in auditors' letters to management; (iv) noncompliance with International Standards on Auditing or equivalent national standards; and (v) poorly trained external auditors. These problems are often exacerbated by a board that is unfamiliar with its responsibility for overseeing reporting or inexperienced in implementing good reporting practices. The result can be that financial reports are unsuitable for decision making and do not allow the government or public to understand the financial sustainability of the SOE.

IFRS compliance is essential.[12] The SOE board must assume the responsibility for ensuring that the preparation of annual financial reports takes place on a timely basis and uses appropriate standards. Financial reports should comply with the International Accounting Standard 20 Accounting for Government Grants and Disclosure. In addition, any PSOs should be disclosed publicly with their associated costs.

Annual reporting should be timely (published within no more than 4 months of fiscal year end) and cover the issues that are most commonly demanded by investors. At a minimum, the annual financial reports should include

- a description of the company, industry, and competitive context;
- audited financial reports including financial position, cash flow, and notes;
- management's discussion and analysis;
- segment information according to IFRS 8 Operating Segments; and
- commercial and policy objectives and specific PSOs.

Beyond financial reporting, SOEs should disclose the same information provided by best practice private sector companies and make such information available on their websites. Generally, this is equivalent to the standards of a company listed on a major market. All disclosures should be made available on SOE websites and be available to the public free of cost.

The Bankable SOE suggests a broad range of data that should inform credit decisions, beyond financial information and PSOs. Other information include

- a clear statement of enterprise objectives and their fulfillment;
- the governance, ownership and voting structure of the enterprise;
- the remuneration of board members and key executives;
- board member qualifications, selection process, including board diversity policies, roles on other company boards and whether members are considered independent;
- material foreseeable risk factors and measures taken to manage risk;

---

[12]   In some countries, national accounting standards may be considered equivalent to IFRS.

- financial assistance, including guarantees, received from the state and commitments made on behalf of the SOE, including contractual commitments and liabilities arising from public–private partnerships;
- material transactions with the state and/or other related entities;
- policies toward accounting and auditing, ethics, and risk; and
- any relevant issues relating to employees and other stakeholders.

Audit and controls

SOEs should have their annual financial reports audited by a reputable independent external auditor using International Standards on Auditing. State audits are not considered a substitute for an independent external audit of an SOE's financial statements. State audits should focus on the use of public funds and can be considered a useful supplement to an independent external audit. In addition, state auditors may be useful in helping identify where the SOE's internal reporting and controls have weaknesses. Qualified opinions by auditors, especially if they are repeated, are a sign of information risk and often indicative of deeper problems.

The SOE should have an audit committee that is staffed by independent board members who are financially literate. The responsibilities of the audit committee should include ensuring that the external auditor remains independent and that management addresses any shortcomings identified by auditors in their letters to management. It is essential that the SOE has a risk management framework overseen by the board. The audit committee often fulfills a risk management oversight function for the board, though a separate risk oversight committee staffed by independent board members may be useful and is generally expected in state-owned financial institutions.

The SOE should have an effective internal audit function. The internal audit function reports to management administratively but should be independent from management. It should have a direct autonomous reporting relationship to the board on substantive issues and, where possible, to a board audit committee staffed wholly by independent and financially literate board members. The internal auditor should have the independence to develop their own internal audit plan with feedback from the board. In addition, the internal auditor should have sufficient capacity. Internal audit should comply with the standards of the Institute of Internal Audit as well as COSO standards. The internal audit function should ensure compliance with and effectiveness of the SOE's internal controls.

It is important for the SOE board to have a good awareness of risk management practices. Good risk management practices should be in place at the operational level. However, what is often overlooked is the degree to which SOE boards exercise oversight of the risk management function. It is not uncommon for SOE boards to lack basic knowledge of risk management. This can pose problems, especially in state-owned banks and insurance firms. It is also a problem more generally given the growing importance attributed by investors to strong risk management and a more expansive consideration of corporate risks. For example, contemporary risk management practices should consider environmental, social, legal, and reputational risks among others. *The Bankable SOE* provides some basic guidance on how to assess SOE risk management practices (*The Bankable SOE*, Table 5).

Conflict of interest and related party transactions

Weaknesses in controls may permit abusive related party transactions to occur. These may cause significant financial and reputational damage to SOEs, and their creditors and shareholders. Unfortunately, they are all too common between SOEs, SOEs and government agencies, and SOEs and private enterprises connected to SOE board and managers as well as politically connected individuals. Examples of abusive transactions include

- selling products or services below fair market value;
- lending at below-market rates, or without repayment;
- exchanging property at nonmarket prices;
- non-collection of receivables from related parties; and
- payment for unnecessary consulting services.

Related party transactions can also be used to distort financial reports and mislead shareholders and creditors.

SOEs should have effective policies for controlling conflicts of interest and potentially abusive related party transactions. Relevant policies may be found in, for example, ethics codes, a responsible business conduct policy, a board charter or bylaws, or a dedicated conflict of interest policy. The key factor to consider when examining implementation of such policies is the "tone at the top," that is, if the board exercises strong and visible leadership in encouraging ethical behavior. Another important consideration is whether the internal auditor reviews the systems that are designed to control conflicts of interest. It is important that rules for regulating conflicts of interest apply to the board and top executives (where power and potential for conflicts are concentrated) and not just staff. Board depoliticization and independence are also important to avoid abusive transactions, and policies and practices on related party transactions should also ensure that transactions with other SOEs are done on an arms-length basis.

The content of conflict-of-interest and related party transactions policies should correspond to good practice standards. Model ethics codes and conflict of interest policies can be found on the websites of professional organizations such as institutes of chartered secretaries, corporate governance associations, and so forth. At a minimum, such policies should require that

- all related party transactions take place at "arm's length,"
- all related party transactions be approved exclusively by independent board members,
- conflicted individuals be recused from decision making,
- board and top management make annual declarations of their interests and potential conflicts and update these immediately when new potential conflicts arise,
- information on the affiliations of board members and top executives where conflicts might arise be published on the SOE's website, and
- all related party transactions over a certain size that occurred during the year be reported (this is normally done when IFRS are properly applied).

Rights of minority shareholders

All of the previous advice in this section can help protect minority shareholders. For those SOEs that are listed, are seeking to list, or otherwise have a growing number of outside shareholders, the SOE and the controlling owner should comply both with the *OECD Guidelines on Corporate Governance of State-Owned Enterprises on State-Owned Enterprises* and the *G20/OECD Principles of Corporate Governance*, which establish best governance practices for listed companies. Chapter 8 of the *Corporate Governance of State-Owned Enterprises: A Toolkit* provide additional guidance on effective treatment of nonstate shareholders.

For both nonlisted and listed SOEs, crucial aspects of the equitable treatment of minority shareholders are (i) equal and simultaneous access to all material information (fair disclosure); (ii) proactive communication by the SOE with nonstate shareholders; (iii) implementation of controls to manage conflicts of interest and related party transactions; (iv) minority shareholder consultation, possible minority representation on boards, and cumulative voting; and (v) effective participation at general shareholders meetings, including the right to nominate and vote on board members and propose resolutions for the agenda. In addition, minority shareholders should benefit from preemptive and tag-along rights that should be enshrined in securities law. It is also essential that shareholders have fair and effective recourse through the judicial system against the SOE and other owners in case their legal rights are infringed. Equal treatment should exist for domestic and international investors, and of course for ADB if it is an equity investor. To facilitate equal treatment and effective communication with shareholders and potential shareholders, the SOE should have a dedicated investor relations function.

Credit rating

One of the most straightforward ways to make an SOE more bankable, and to find out how bankable it is, is for it to be rated by one or more international credit rating agencies. Alternatives to this include ratings from national credit rating agencies and shadow credit ratings. The latter are not made public and can indicate ways to improve creditworthiness. All the guidance in this section and the next can help an SOE improve its credit rating.

Government commitment and credibility

To credibly access commercial finance, an SOE must be financially sustainable and able to operate with sufficient autonomy and efficiency. These ultimately depend on the government and government policy. Will commitments to raise tariffs or inject equity hold, or be reversed? Can the government operate through normal shareholder and policy mechanisms, or will the SOE be subject to ongoing micromanaging and political interference? Will action be taken if the board and senior management consistently underperform, or will they keep their positions for other reasons?

A lack of credibility can hinder the performance of the SOE and make it unbankable. However, the government may also lack credibility when removing a sovereign guarantee and allowing the SOE to borrow on its own. In implicit guarantee—the belief that the government will bail out the SOE, and specifically its creditors, even if no formal guarantee is given—can create comfort for creditors, but it is also a source of moral hazard that can undermine SOE reform and the benefits of the SOE accessing commercial finance. And, as the *Bankable SOE* makes clear, SOEs do default and creditors do lose money, sometimes in spectacular fashion.[13]

Ensuring government credibility and improving SOE access to commercial finance may require broader reforms. These are discussed next.

---

[13] For example, the Fannie Mae case study in ADB. 2022. *Governance of State-Owned Enterprises (SOEs): Cases for Capacity Development Programs.* Manila.

Broader Reforms and Risk Factors for Commercial Finance of State-Owned Enterprises

There are many factors that influence the bankability of an SOE beyond its specific governance or financial performance. These factors often depend on government policy and hence increase the risk for any or several SOE borrowers in a particular country, region, or municipality. These potential risks also create reform opportunities that can help an SOE or SOEs access commercial finance, with the corresponding benefits to those SOEs and the government's fiscal position.

Teams looking at potential NSOs should also be aware of the risks and reform opportunities noted here. If these risks are suspected, staff in PSOD should reach out to regional department colleagues in the relevant sectors as well as the resident missions. They can also help in upstream reform.

Policy-based lending and/or the provision of TA can be effective tools to support broader reform. Furthermore, ADB has knowledge of and experience with SOE governance from other countries that can inform this reform. Such experience can be invaluable in developing potential solutions. The *Guidance Note on State-Owned Enterprise Reform in Sovereign Projects and Programs* has more on using policy-based lending to support SOE reform. The other references in Box 1 provide more in-depth guidance on broader SOE reform. For national and sector reform, this includes *Corporate Governance of State-Owned Enterprises: A Toolkit*, Chapters 2 through 5 and Appendixes A and B. *The Bankable SOE* also discusses these broader reforms in the context of access to commercial finance.

Country risk

Country risk encompasses the potential for sovereign default, and factors that could affect sovereign or commercial creditworthiness. *The Bankable SOE* illustrates how ratings for country risk can be assigned based on performance against key indicators (*The Bankable SOE*, Table 6). In the case of Fitch Ratings, country risk is defined as a function of (i) economic environment, (ii) financial system development, and (iii) country governance. The governance component is further subdivided into (i) rule of law; (ii) government effectiveness; and (iii) issues such as corruption, regulatory quality, political stability, voice, and accountability (*The Bankable SOE*, Table 7).

One implication is that broad reforms to raise the sovereign credit rating, or improve the overall climate for borrowing, can also help bring down SOE borrowing costs and improve access to finance. This could include, for example, more effective regulation of the banking sector, or steps to improve rule of law indicators.

Country risk has an asymmetric relationship with SOE credit ratings. Typically, the credit rating of a financially weak SOE does not improve because of a strong country rating. On the other hand, the rating of a financially strong SOE will only rarely exceed that of a weaker country rating. In summary, SOEs will not generally have a better credit rating than the DMC though they can always have a worse credit rating.

Competitive neutrality

An uneven "playing field" between SOEs and the private sector can create unfair conditions for competition. Countries may assert that competitive neutrality between private companies and SOEs exists but, in practice, it is common for a web of visible and invisible anti-competitive practices to persist. *The Bankable SOE* identifies potential challenges to competitive neutrality from the perspective of regulation, taxation, procurement, financing, and compensation mechanisms.

Some of the differences that confer advantages and disadvantages to SOEs are shown in Table 1.

Table 1: Competitive Neutrality

Possible advantages for SOEs	Possible disadvantages for SOEs
Regulation	
• Monopoly rights	• Bureaucracy, inability to innovate, and act flexibly and rapidly
• Exemptions from competition law, fees, and/or environmental standards	• Weak governance practices including undue political intervention, weak accountability for politicians and boards
• Less stringent disclosure and transparency practices compared to private reporting	• Boards and executives that lack needed business and other skills
• Easier access to land or approvals	• Unstable leadership due to politically driven changes in boards and management
• Implicit and explicit protection against lawsuits including insolvency	• Public sector labor and pay practices, inability to incentivize staff through pay or promotion, low staff morale, overstaffing and inability to rationalize staff
	• Vulnerability to corruption, nepotism, weaker controls
	• Significant additional reporting burdens to government and additional audits
Taxation	
• Tax preferences and rights to collect fees or levy special taxes (e.g., airports)	• Additional taxes levied specifically on SOE operations
Procurement	
• Preferential pricing of some key inputs such as energy, water, land, facilities rentals	• Rigid public procurement rules, forced procurement from other SOEs or authorized providers who may be more costly
• Advantages over private sector in government procurement	
Financing	
• Privileged access to finance, implicit (if not explicit) guarantees for borrowing	• Mandatory borrowing from state lenders, limitations on borrowing or accessing finance
• Too big or too important to fail, especially in the banking sector, i.e., final state backstop	• Mandatory deposits with state banks
• No requirement to have a return on capital	
Compensation Mechanisms	
	• PSOs that are not fully compensated, inability to charge back full costs, and lack of independent tariff setting
	• Poor collections for regulated services (toleration of consumer nonpayment)

PSO = public sector obligation, SOE = state-owned enterprise.

Source: Asian Development Bank. 2021. *The Bankable SOE: Commercial Financing for State-Owned Enterprises.* Manila.

Governments may subject SOEs to differential treatment at any time and may reverse or remove certain benefits. This makes it difficult to forecast future cash flows and repayment capacity and even the viability of an SOE. The best indicator of whether SOEs are vulnerable to the risk of intervention tends to be the past behavior of a government though, as with financial reports, past actions are not always a reliable indicator.

While perceptions are often that SOEs are favored over the private sector, differing competitive conditions can also make it more difficult for SOEs to operate effectively and efficiently. Whether SOEs or the private sector have the advantage is not the central question. The goal is to encourage governments to level the playing field between SOEs and the private sector to the maximum extent possible to ensure fair conditions for both sides.

SOEs seeking commercial finance should generally seek to have as few differences with private sector companies as possible. In general, they should have the same corporate form, fall under the same regulations, and be taxed the same way. When special policy or noncommercial goals are mandated for an SOE, they should be addressed through a system of PSOs.

Public service obligations

The provision of PSOs can constitute a legitimate rationale for state ownership. Formal PSOs are also an important element of ensuring a level playing field with the private sector; however, poorly specified PSOs and withholding compensation for the costs of PSOs are two of the most significant challenges to SOE performance. Remedies to the problem include the following:

- **Compensation for PSOs** can be improved by formal contracting with the government.
- **Performance** can be enhanced by linking the PSO to output and other service delivery indicators.
- **Transparency** can promote compliance: the essential expectations under a PSO and related subsidies should be publicly disclosed.
- **Accounting for PSOs** helps clarify the real costs. SOEs can be required to maintain separate accounts for PSOs and related activities versus commercial activities.

Related reforms can make PSOs more effective while also addressing competitive neutrality:

- **Cost recovery** can be achieved by better cost management and improved billing and collections. Fair tariff setting can be achieved by establishing technically competent and truly independent tariff setters in line with international standards of best practice.
- **Financing advantages** can be discouraged by governments who can mandate that loans from government entities to SOEs should be at market rates. Additionally, SOEs may be required to pay a competitive neutrality fee if they pay lower-than-market rates on their debt.
- **Procurement** can be enhanced by requiring SOEs to certify that they are compliant with competitive neutrality principles. Abnormally low tenders can be disqualified when they result from an advantage due to government ownership.

In practice, implementing such remedies for PSOs and competitive neutrality may be subject to significant political economy constraints. For example, governments may want to require SOEs to procure from other SOEs or state entities to support them. In addition, it may be difficult to provide full compensation when a government has weak public finances and wishes to externalize its costs.

When substantive reforms face challenges, disclosure of PSOs can be an easier but effective step forward. In line with the OECD *Guidelines on Corporate Governance of State-Owned Enterprises*, SOEs should publicly disclose information on PSOs. Reporting on PSOs helps lenders, equity investors, and the public assess their true costs. The reporting of PSOs is particularly important for establishing clear and transparent financing mechanisms for noncommercial functions.

Sector issues

SOEs often operate in regulated or monopolistic sectors, where sector regulation and governance can have a significant impact on performance and bankability. In these cases, the roles of policy maker, regulator, and state owner should be as separate as possible. Regulated prices—also known as tariffs—should be set by an independent regulator or through an objective and independent process. They should ensure that an SOE operating in an adequate manner can cover both operational and capital costs, including depreciation. PSOs should be used to cover the expense of providing a service at a loss, for example nonrevenue water and sewage, rural electricity distribution, or air or ferry service to remote areas. Health, safety, and environmental factors may be included in regulation and service requirements, but these must also be reflected in tariffs and PSO provision.

If the SOE has a monopoly, then in some cases competition with the private sector can be encouraged, for example in electricity production or banking. This includes those cases where an SOE was established to catalyze an industry, but now others could enter the field. Capacity building in the SOE and ensuring that the playing field remains level for both the SOE and private sector may be needed as the SOE transitions to a competitive environment. Other ways of encouraging the private sector are described below.

Professionalizing state-owned enterprise oversight

Those in the government responsible for SOE oversight should act in a professional matter and have the needed skills and objectivity. One way to ensure professional oversight is to have a specialized body responsible for overseeing SOEs that is separate from other bodies that make policy or regulate the relevant sector. Sometimes this is a coordinating body that works with other ministries. The most effective are focused ownership entities that carry out the various shareholder functions in an SOE independently from the rest of government. This is sometimes called the "centralized" approach. This is typically a specialized agency or holding company. There may be one such entity for all the SOEs under a particular government, or there may be more than one, for example one specializing in state-owned banks, and another for nonfinancial SOEs. In many cases, more commercial SOEs will be with the ownership entity, while noncommercial corporatized entities will remain different government ministries.[14]

Centralized oversight permits the owner to take a holistic view of the SOE sector and implement SOE policy efficiently for the entire sector. In addition, an ownership entity can provide a financial and performance-orientated shareholder perspective. An ownership entity also permits a better separation between the policy and regulatory functions of the state versus the responsibilities of the state as a shareholder, and thus serves to manage the conflicts of interest that can arise from combining these functions. Such an entity can also help reduce the scope for political interference and bring greater professionalism to the state's ownership role by pooling specialized capabilities and scarce resources.

---

[14]   This does not include the central bank or independent regulatory entities that may have a corporate form and operate independently from the rest of the government. These are not considered SOEs for the purpose of this guidance note.

An ownership policy is an essential document that guides the ownership entity and the state in its governance of SOEs. The ownership policy should include an ownership rationale for SOEs. The rationale lays out the criteria for deciding which SOEs should remain in state hands and which should not. The basic presumption of a good ownership rationale is that the default position is for commercial activities to be provided by the private sector. The state should own commercial operations only when there is a market failure, where the operation is of strategic interest to the state, or where there is an infant industries argument.

The state should exercise its ownership rights via the normal channels provided under company law. Generally, the state shareholder should follow private sector norms and limit its engagement to attending shareholder meetings and voting the state's shares, setting up merit-based board nominations and appointments, and monitoring board and SOE performance. In addition, the state shareholder should ensure that the SOE's governance practices are sound, including ensuring proper board composition, that reporting systems and disclosure are adequate, and that board compensation is sufficient to attract qualified candidates.

One of the most important functions of the state shareholder is board nomination and appointment. The process for selecting board members should be formal, apolitical, and transparent, and aim at securing the best talent for the SOE. To reduce undue political influence, countries may delegate part of the board member nominations process to an independent nominations commission or an independent ownership entity. A nominations committee of the SOE board, chaired by an independent board member and consisting only of independent board members, can help define the experience and skills needs of the board and communicate these to a nominations commission or the ownership entity. The development of a pool or database of prequalified board candidates by the state can facilitate nominations.

The social goals of the state should be implemented by the SOE board and SOE management and not the state via direct intervention in the SOE's operations. The state should not involve itself in the day–to-day management of the SOE. Rather, the state should contract PSOs with the SOE and entrust the board and executives with their implementation. This formalizes interactions with the SOE and insulates the SOE from micromanagement, politicization, and informality in decision making. It also removes the ultimate responsibility for SOE performance from the state and assigns it to boards and executives. This places the state in its proper role of guiding, monitoring, and holding the SOE accountable.

The ownership entity should help establish KPIs in cooperation with the SOE and use them to monitor performance. As noted, these can include measures of returns on equity and profitability as well other financial indicators (*The Bankable SOE* Chapter IV.A. has more on financial indicators for SOEs). Other KPIs may include measures of operational efficiency, service delivery, and relevant ESG indicators.

Privatization and private sector engagement

Successful privatization will require many of the previously noted steps and accessing commercial finance may be a planned or fortuitous first step toward privatization. SOEs that have been reformed are also generally in a better position to effectively deal with the private sector on a professional and arm's length basis. In addition to access to finance, this also includes engaging with the private sector through procurement and outsourcing. Contracting out more functions with the private sector can improve SOE efficiency, and, if the SOE has a significant presence in the economy, encourage private sector development. However, such contracting should be transparent and avoid conflicts of interest. The ADB *Guidance Note on State-Owned Enterprise Reform in Sovereign Projects and Programs* and the ADB *Governance Brief: Privatization Today*, have more on effective privatization of SOEs.

One ADB Projects with State-Owned Enterprises

The One ADB approach allows ADB's regional departments and PSOD to work together on a transaction, including transactions with SOEs. This approach, and specifically using it to prepare SOEs for commercial financing, is a strategic priority for ADB.[15] By bringing together the sector and policy expertise of the regional departments with the commercial and transaction experience of PSOD, this approach is especially suited to supporting SOE reform. However, it also requires a collaborative approach and a willingness by both the team and the counterpart to make the changes needed for bankability.

ADB has issued a Framework for One ADB Nonsovereign Public Sector Financing, to be used by staff in PSOD and the regional departments working together.[16] Its focus is joint work across departments, primarily with SOEs, and all such joint teams should refer to it.

The framework emphasizes the necessity of continued reform of SOEs to support their development into managerially and financially autonomous entities, capable of borrowing on nonsovereign terms. Other principles include the importance of policy dialogue about SOEs and their role and the importance of phasing out government financial support to SOEs so they can emerge as commercially viable entities. A level playing field with the private sector should also be supported, including through moving SOEs from sovereign financing to commercial financing.

Joint teams should have leaders from each department. Appendix 1 of the framework provides a detailed breakdown of primary roles and responsibilities, with the processing steps that PSOD team members should focus on, and those that regional department team members should focus on. These are aligned with the relative strengths and processing approaches of the respective departments.

The framework is intended for NSO transactions originated and identified by the regional departments. The implied logic is that many potential clients for joint processing will be SOEs that had relied on sovereign loans from ADB—processed by the regional departments—and are now interested in moving to nonsovereign finance, at their own initiating or at the behest of their government. In other cases, the government may come to ADB through the regional department for an SOE that has not been a (recent) borrower and is now seeking commercial finance. Even when the loan is initiated by PSOD, the framework is still useful guidance for One ADB teams.

There are important differences between sovereign and nonsovereign financing terms, structure, and approach. For example, commercial borrowers normally have to bear some of the cost of due diligence, and the details of due diligence, loan negotiations, and loan covenants will be different in the case of commercial borrowing.

---

[15] ADB. 2018. *Strategy 2030: Achieving a Prosperous, Resilient, Inclusive, and Sustainable Asia and the Pacific.* Manila. para. 79; and ADB. 2019. *Operational Plan for Private Sector Operations, 2019–2024.* Manila.

[16] ADB. 2019. Framework for Joint Processing by Private Sector Operations Department and Regional Departments for Nonsovereign Public Sector Financing Transactions Identified and/or Originated by Regional Departments. 17 January.

Perhaps more significantly, the absence of a sovereign guarantee brings further attention to the need to identify and mitigate commercial risks. All this serves as a learning experience for the SOE and its management.

It is not just SOE management that faces a learning curve. PSOD and the regional departments do work differently. Staff typically have different skill sets, and there are important differences in processing and focus. These are why a One ADB approach can add value beyond a normal transaction, but also why patience is a needed attribute of One ADB team members.

Supporting the Transition to Nonsovereign Borrowing

The One ADB approach is appropriate for SOEs that cannot easily borrow on commercial terms, either from PSOD or the market, but could move to such borrowing with the right reform. The SOE counterpart may have relied primarily or exclusively on sovereign guarantees and is now moving to commercial finance. There may be good reasons for this, but is typically more expensive, with a higher interest rate and fees.

Both aspects of this transition need to be considered. SOE reform is certainly required in these projects and should be a primary focus (footnote 11). This should include a review of the risk and reform areas noted here, and steps to address those that could affect bankability. Some SOEs that are seeking commercial finance for the first time may also have more fundamental problems that must be addressed. The ADB *Guidance Note on State-Owned Enterprise Reform in Sovereign Projects and Programs* covers additional risk and reform areas, including asset maintenance, and human resources and restructuring, that may be relevant. It also has terms of reference for consultants to support SOE reform, and a questionnaire to supplement the information gathering normally done as part of sovereign projects.[17]

In some cases, it may be too soon to move to NSO financing. A sovereign project or program and TA under the regional department may be the best options to move the SOE closer to commercial viability. The ADB *Guidance Note on State-Owned Enterprise Reform in Sovereign Projects and Programs* remains the primary reference in this case, with *The Bankable SOE* and this note providing additional guidance for steps to improve creditworthiness.

While upstream work may be led by the regional department, if the focus is commercial orientation, then it may be worthwhile to include PSOD staff in the project team. And while the framework may focus on work originating with the regional departments, in some cases PSOD may identify an SOE that needs more upstream work and in turn bring that work to the regional departments, with the understanding that it may lead to a future NSO. In addition, the Office of Public–Private Partnership may also find viable candidates in its work and help with related commercialization.

For SOEs that are close to bankability, ADB teams have taken a few different approaches to support the transition to commercial borrowing, including ways of least partially offsetting the higher cost. These include substantial technical assistance, a partial sovereign guarantee, and combining sovereign lending with NSO in the same project. These approaches are described next, each with an ADB project example that took that approach.

---

[17] For regular ADB sovereign borrowers, there may be extensive past financial and financial finanagment information that can help identify potential risk and reform areas for commercial borrowing.

Substantial technical assistance

TA can and should be used to identify and address the main reform needs and risks of the SOE, with a focus to enhance creditworthiness. This will build the capacity of the SOE and its staff for the NSO transaction while supporting reforms with a development impact. To the extent that it can increase bankability, it may also allow for borrowing on better terms. TA can also be added to the approaches noted next.

Example ADB project: Climate-Resilient and Smart Urban Water Infrastructure Project (People's Republic of China).

Partial sovereign guarantee

A government can provide a guarantee to what is otherwise an NSO transaction if a failure to honor the guarantee does not trigger cross-default on other ADB loans to that DMC.[18] Such a guarantee may be issued by a national government that is a regular ADB borrower on a special basis, with an explicit and legally binding provision agreed by both parties. Or it may be with a provincial or municipal government, where ADB sovereign loans have guarantees by the national government, and no such provision is given in this case.

When there is such a guarantee it may be an NSO, but it is not a standard one. SOE reform must be there (footnote 11) and a One ADB approach followed. The framework should be used, or used as guidance if the loan is originated by PSOD. In turn, the borrower should be as financially viable as any other seeking an NSO loan—the goal is very much not to need the guarantee, and the borrower should also undergo standard NSO due diligence, including for corporate governance. If credible, the guarantee can increase the creditworthiness of the borrower and lead to a lower cost, however the cost of the loan may still be higher than under a full sovereign guarantee.

Example ADB project: Kochi Metro Extension Project (India).

Combining sovereign and nonsovereign lending

Under this approach, a single integrated project has two loans—one sovereign and one nonsovereign.[19] This brings the average cost of the project down from a pure NSO loan, while not adding as much to public debt as a pure sovereign loan. It also facilitates the transition to full commercial borrowing. For this approach to be successful, the government commitment must be clear, and the package agreed to as a whole. The benefits of the NSO component must be understood, as it will have a higher cost to the borrower than the sovereign component and involve different procedures—though these procedures will help the borrower prepare for commercial borrowing.

Example ADB project: Bengaluru Smart Energy Efficient Power Distribution Project (India).

All of the above are very much possible under current ADB practices and procedures, and each has been used successfully. Another possibility, similar to combining sovereign and nonsovereign lending, would be to combine a grant with an NSO. In this case, ADB's procedures for blended finance should be adhered to.[20] Other approaches have been proposed and may be possible. One such proposal is in Box 2.

---

[18]   "Nonsovereign operations comprise the provision of any loan, guarantee, equity investment, or other financing arrangement to privately held, state-owned, or subsovereign entities, in each case, (i) without a government guarantee; or (ii) with a government guarantee, under terms that do not allow ADB, upon default by the guarantor, to accelerate, suspend, or cancel any other loan or guarantee between ADB and the related sovereign." ADB. 2019. *Staff Instruction on Credit and other processes for Nonsovereign Operations.* Manila; and footnote 1.

[19]   The sovereign loan may be made (i) to the government which then onlends it to the SOE or (ii) directly to the SOE with a sovereign guarantee. The nonsovereign will be made directly to the SOE, with no guarantee.

[20]   ADB. 2020. *Staff Instruction on Procedures for Endorsement of ADB Blended Concessional Finance Proposals.* Manila.

Box 2: The Stand-by Facility

The Stand-by Facility is a proposed way to combine sovereign and nonsovereign financing. It involves a variable guarantee and can achieve an effective credit rating and interest rate that lies between those for full sovereign and full nonsovereign.

The facility involves the following steps:

(i)   ADB (potentially with other commercial cofinanciers) provides a funded nonsovereign loan to an SOE and a sovereign loan to the sovereign. The sovereign loan's terms offer an availability period approximate to the tenor of the nonsovereign loan.

(ii) Simultaneously, the sovereign enters into a subordinated subsidiary loan agreement with the SOE in the same principal amount and on the same tenor as the sovereign loan.

(iii) If the SOE misses a principal or interest payment, ADB, acting under an agency agreement (as agent of the sovereign and the SOE), draws down on both the sovereign loan and subordinated subsidiary loans and (as agent of the SOE) makes the payment due to ADB (and any cofinanciers) under the NSO loan.

(iv) The sovereign repays ADB for any sovereign loan drawdowns, and the SOE (a) on a senior footing repays outstanding principal under the nonsovereign loan and (b) on a basis subordinated in cash flow terms to its senior debt, repays the principal drawn under the subordinated subsidiary loan agreement with the sovereign.

Under the facility, the loan to the SOE is entirely nonsovereign but has effectively received a guarantee back up by a sovereign loan to the DMC. Typically, the guarantee will be less than 100%, and the interest rate will reflect the size of the guarantee. By lowering the guarantee, the sovereign exposure will go down, but the direct cost to the SOE will go up.

TRANSACTION EXAMPLE
Assumptions:
Borrower: Indian SOE
Principal: $100 million
Tenor: 10 years
Credit rating: Equivalent to BBB–
Repayment schedule: Semiannual

Pricing
Original credit rating	BBB–	BBB–	BBB–	BBB–
Stand-by facility first-loss coverage (a)	30.6%	26.2%	20.5%	13.8%
Enhanced credit rating	≥A	A–	BBB+	BBB
Credit spread (b)	1.16%	1.22%	1.29%	1.37%
Commitment fee (c)	0.15%	0.15%	0.15%	0.15%
Hybrid price ($b + ac$)	1.21%	1.26%	1.32%	1.39%

Reference Pricing
Sovereign price	0.50%	0.50%	0.50%	0.50%
Nonsovereign price	1.51%	1.51%	1.51%	1.51%

ADB = Asian Development Bank, DMC = developing member country, NSO = nonsovereign operation, SOE = state-owned enterprise.
Source: Donald Lambert, principal private sector development specialist, ADB.

Conclusion

Building State-Owned Enterprise Reform into Nonsovereign Operations and One ADB Transactions

To build SOE reform into an ADB NSO, start at or before the concept stage. Learn what previous SOE reforms and TA projects have been carried out in the relevant SOE or sector. Commit to a dialogue with the counterpart to establish the importance and usefulness of SOE reform, including access to commercial finance, and find common ground on the reforms that will be supported. If broader or more challenging risks are identified, then the regional department may need to take the lead through sovereign operations or TA. Broader discussions on national SOE reform should also be linked to the country partnership strategy process, and when relevant, included in the country partnership strategy.[21] Critically, substantial SOE reform will require a champion in the SOE or in government, and that champion should be supported through ADB's engagement.

If the known risks are judged manageable, the transaction can proceed. The concept review form or concept paper should briefly introduce and describe the SOE and identify a few areas where reform may be needed. Next, use due diligence, to understand possible challenges in more detail and identify unforeseen challenges at the concept stage.

Based on these findings, use the advice in this note and, if needed, the references in Box 1, to develop proposed reforms. In each case, try to find a TA that can help the proposed reforms to be implemented. A diverse team—including legal and financial management specialists as well as specialists and officers from the regional department and resident mission—can help in developing these reforms.

There is no need to address all the areas noted here, or all the potential weaknesses identified. As indicated in Strategy 2030, SOE reform should improve service delivery and move the SOE to accessing nonsovereign finance. Importantly, broader SOE reform can also improve the quality and viability of transactions for multiple SOEs in a particular DMC. Box 3 summarizes the steps for NSO with SOEs. The appendix summarizes the criteria that SOEs should meet to access commercial finance.

Under the SOE Working Group, ADB provides ongoing training and information sharing on SOE reform for staff and DMC officials. This training can provide greater comfort with the material presented here and new perspectives on SOE challenges and opportunities. Help is also available through the governance team in ADB's Sustainable Development and Climate Change Department, either through ADB staff or recommended consultants. Bringing a specialist in early on for the project or program can be one of the best ways to enhance SOE reform.

---

[21]   ADB. 2018. *Management Response to Thematic Evaluation on State-Owned Enterprise Engagement and Reform*. Manila.

Box 3: Summary Steps for Nonsovereign Operation with State-Owned Enterprises

1) **As part of country programing, identify potential SOEs interested in nonsovereign operations.** The demand may come from the SOE or government, but government support is always needed.

2) **Conduct an initial identification of potential risk and reforms.** Take advantage of existing program documentation and staff who may be familiar with the SOE.

3) **Determine if commercial borrowing is possible.** Based on analysis in step 2:

   - If reforms needed for commercial borrowing are impossible or unlikely, NSO is ruled out. Sovereign lending may still be possible.

   - If commercial borrowing requires broader and or longer-term reform, support through sovereign projects and or regional department TA will be needed. Afterward, return to step 2.

   - If commercial borrowing is possible with shorter term reforms, go to step 4.

4) **Determine if it will be a standard NSO or One ADB approach.** If any of the following hold true, a One ADB approach should be used:

   - The project is initiated by the regional department.

   - The project will involve significant TA, which may come from the regional department.

   - The project involves partial sovereign guarantee, combines sovereign lending with NSO, combines grants with NSO, or uses another approach that combines NSO with alternative financing equivalent to sovereign financing.

   Otherwise, a standard NSO may be used.

5) **Process the transaction.** Continue to be aware of and identify potential SOE-related risk, including through the due diligence stage. As needed, utilize available TA and staff that can address financial, sector, or governance issues if they arise. Capture SOE challenges and reform in the RRP.

6) **After the transaction.** Support important ongoing reform through financial covenants, monitoring and supervision, and by connecting to other TA and projects and programs that may be relevant. If it is an equity investment, ongoing dialogue and exercise of shareholder functions will be crucial to ensure that good governance is maintained.

7) **Next steps.** Can the SOE be made even more creditworthy? Can it issue bonds or equity? Is there interest in privatization? Can lessons from this transaction by used for another transaction? What broader policy changes would support SOE commercial finance in the DMC? Consider ways to continue supporting ADB's strategic priority of providing commercial finance to SOEs.

ADB = Asian Development Bank, DMC = developing member country, NSO = nonsovereign operations, RRP = report and recommendation of the President, SOE = state-owned enterprise, TA = technical assistance.

Source: Asian Development Bank.

Appendix: Criteria for Nonsovereign Operations with State-Owned Enterprises

This section summarizes the risk and reform considerations for nonsovereign operations (NSOs) with state-owned enterprises (SOEs) given in sections V and VI. Those sections should be read carefully to place this summary criteria in context and understand related risk and possible reforms to ensure that the criteria are in place by the time the transaction is completed.

Table A1: State-Owned Enterprise Risk and Reform in Nonsovereign Operations (Section V)

Area	Criteria
Cash Flow and Financial Performance	• SOE generates sufficient cashflow[a] • SOE is profitable[a] • SOE has financial targets[a] • SOE pays dividends[b] • SOE has a disclosed dividend policy[b]
Financial Structure	• SOE has a sustainable debt to equity ratio[a] • SOE issues securities on capital markets[b]
Focus and Ownership Structure	• SOE has a clear mandate[a] • SOE noncore functions do not threaten cash flow or profitability[a] • SOE ownership understood[a] • Major state-linked counterparties clear[a] • Credible commitment to focus on core activities[a] • SOE restructured to remove noncore functions[b] • SOE ownership consolidated, simplified[b]
Board Role and Functions	• Board influences selection of CEO and can hold CEO accountable[a] • Board oversees SOE strategy[a] • Board performs other key functions[a] • Board members have a clear obligation to act in the interest of the SOE[a] • Board has supporting structures and practices[b] • Board role and practices consistent with attracting equity investment[b]

continued on next page

Table A1   *continued*

Area	Criteria
Board Composition and Independence	• Board has necessary skills and knowledge[a] • Board has sufficient independence and objectivity[a] • Board is not subject to informal or undue political interference[a] • Board has independent member(s) who are not civil servants[a] • Board has five to eight members, most of whom are nonexecutive and independent of government[b]
Disclosure	• SOE issues IFRS or equivalent financial statements[a] • Financial statements are timely[a] • Discloses mandate, broad objectives, and material PSOs[a] • Discloses nonfinancial information consistent with local listed companies and international good practice[b]
Audit and Controls	• Qualified external auditor and audit in compliance with ISA[a] • Independent and qualified board member(s) oversee audit[a] • SOE has an internal audit function[a] • SOE has a risk management function[a] • Independent and qualified board member(s) oversee risk management[b]
Conflict of interest and related party transactions	• Transactions with other SOEs done at an arm's length and market basis[a] • Code of ethics and/or other policies address potential conflicts of interest involving board members and senior management[a] • Conflicted individuals are recused from relevant decisions[a] • International good practice for conflicts of interest and related party transactions is followed[b] • Independent board members approve related party transactions.[b]
Rights of Minority Shareholders	• All shareholders have equal access to information[b] • Minority shareholders are consulted on major decisions and can influence board composition[b] • Active communication with shareholders and an investor relations function[b] • Shareholder rights under the SOE charter and/or relevant law are consistent with good international practice[b]
Credit Rating	• SOE receives a shadow credit rating or rating from a local agency[b] • SOE rated by one or more international credit rating agencies[b]
Government Commitment and Credibility	• The government is credible in its commitments to the SOE and SOE reform[a] • The government is credible in requiring and allowing the SOE to borrow on commercial terms, and applies no implicit guarantee to such borrowing[a]

CEO = chief executive officer, IFRS = International Financing Reporting Standards, ISA = International Standards on Auditing, NSO = nonsovereign operations, PSO = public sector obligation, SOE = state-owned enterprise.

[a] An essential criterion for NSO to the SOE. The NSO should only proceed if this is met.

[b] Criteria that could increase the creditworthiness and financial sustainability of the SOE.

Source: Asian Development Bank.

Table A2: Broader Reforms and Risk Factors for State-Owned Enterprise Commercial Finance (Section VI)

Area	Criteria
Country Risk	• The government credit rating is high enough to allow commercial borrowing by the SOE[a] • Rule of law strengthened[b] • Financial systems strengthened[b]
Competitive Neutrality	• SOE has a legal form consistent with commercial borrowing[a] • SOE does not depend on subsidies or financial support from the government which may be suddenly removed[a] • SOE operates in a legal and regulatory environment comparable to the private sector[b] • No material difference in SOE taxation compared to private sector companies[b] • No material difference in SOE access to finance compared to private sector companies[b]
Public Service Obligations	• SOE is sufficiently compensated for any government assignments, mandates, or obligations[a] • PSOs are transparent[a] • SOE accounting separates PSO from other activity[a] • PSOs are linked to performance[b] • The government has a national system for SOE PSOs[b]
Sector Issues	• SOE regulated prices/tariffs cover all relevant costs[a] • Pricing and other regulation implemented in an objective manner[a] • State ownership, policy making, and regulation are formally separated[b]
Professionalizing SOE Oversight	• SOE oversight is carried out in a professional and objective manner[a] • SOE oversight prevents informal and undue political interference[a] • There is a specialized part of the government that oversees the SOE[b] • All ownership functions in the SOE are exercised by a dedicated agency or holding company[b] • The government has an ownership policy for SOEs[b]
Privatization and Private Sector Engagement	• SOEs being prepared for possible privatization have suitable legal form and commercial orientation[b] • SOE contracts functions to the private sector in a transparent and arms-length basis[b]

NSO = nonsovereign operations, PSO = public sector obligation, SOE = state-owned enterprise.

[a] An essential criterion for NSO to the SOE. The NSO should only proceed if this is met.

[b] Criteria that could increase the creditworthiness and financial sustainability of the SOE.

Source: Asian Development Bank.

Bibliography

Andrés, L. A., J.L. Guasch, and S. López Azumendi. 2011. Governance in State-Owned Enterprises Revisited: The Cases of Water and Electricity in Latin America and the Caribbean. Policy Research Working Paper. No. 5747. Washington, DC: The World Bank.

Asian Development Bank (ADB). 2018. Financial Due Diligence for Financial Intermediaries. Technical Guidance Note. Manila.

———. 2018. *Strategy 2030: Achieving a Prosperous, Resilient, Inclusive, and Sustainable Asia and the Pacific*. Manila.

———. 2018. *Management Response to Thematic Evaluation on State-Owned Enterprise Engagement and Reform*. Manila.

———. Independent Evaluation Department. 2018. *Thematic Evaluation: State-Owned Enterprise Engagement and Reform*. Manila.

———. 2020. Guidance Note on State-Owned Enterprise Reform in Sovereign Projects and Programs. Manila.

———. 2021. *Guidance Note on State-Owned Enterprise Reform in Sovereign Projects and Programs.* Manila.

Baum, A. et al. 2019. Governance and State-Owned Enterprises: How Costly is Corruption? *IMF Working Paper*. No. 19/253. Washington, DC: International Monetary Fund.

Claessens, S. and B. Yurtoglu. 2012. Corporate Governance and Development–An Update. *Global Corporate Governance Forum Focus* 10. Washington, DC: International Monetary Fund.

Detter, D. 2019. Public Commercial Assets: The Hidden Goldmine. *The Governance Brief*. Issue 40. Manila. : Asian Development Bank.

Detter, D. and S. Fölster. 2015. *Public Wealth of Nations: How Management of Public Assets Can Boost or Bust Economic Growth*. London: UK Palgrave Macmillan.

Jishnu, D. 2005. Reassessing Conditional Cash Transfer Programs. *The World Bank Research Observer.* 20 (1). pp. 57–80.

International Monetary Fund. 2020. *Fiscal Monitor, April 2020: Policies to Support People During the COVID-19 Pandemic*. Washington, DC.

Mako, W. 2021. *The Bankable SOE: Commercial Financing for State-Owned Enterprises*. Manila: ADB.

Organisation for Economic Co-operation and Development (OECD). 2012. *Competitive Neutrality: Maintaining a Level Playing Field between Public and Private Business*. Paris.

———. 2015. *OECD Guidelines on Corporate Governance of State-Owned Enterprises*. Paris.

———. 2019. *Ownership and Governance of State-Owned Enterprises: A Compendium of National Practices*. Paris.

Quality Infrastructure Investment Partnership. 2019. G20 Principles for Quality Infrastructure Investment. Washington, DC.

World Bank. 2014. *Corporate Governance of State-Owned Enterprises: A Toolkit*. October.

World Bank. 2017. *Who Sponsors Infrastructure Projects? Disentangling Public and Private Contributions*. Washington, DC.